Fire Tongue

Zvi A. Sesling

Červená Barva Press
Somerville, Massachusetts

I0079228

Červená Barva Press
P.O. Box 440357
W. Somerville, MA 02144-3222

www.cervenabarvapress.com

Bookstore: www.thelostbookshelf.com

Cover art: Irene Koronas

Cover design: William J. Kelle

Author photo: Susan J. Dechter

Production: Mikail Jaikaran

ISBN: 978-0-9966894-4-1

Library of Congress Control Number: 2016931064

ACKNOWLEDGMENTS

Some of these poems appeared in the following online or print journals. I extend my gratitude to the editors.

Black Heart
Constellations
Ibbetson Street
Littéraire Levure (France)
Sketchbook
The Orange Room Review
Paradise Review
poetry of boston
Wilderness House Literary Review

Thank you to Gloria Mindock, publisher of Červená Barva Press for her support of my writing, Doug Holder of Ibbetson Street Press and Irene Koronas whose support and encouragement has been so important to me. Thank you especially to my wife Susan J. Dechter whose unerring eyes help make these poems readable.

TABLE OF CONTENTS

I. Fire Tongue

II. City

III. Sorrow Road

IV. War Zones

Always for Susan

I. Fire Tongue

Fire Tongue

They called her Fire Tongue,
not for the juicy stick that
entered your mouth all the
way to the throat, but for the
hot spears of words fired like
Apache arrows to the heart

No mercy when angry, no care
for embarrassment for herself
or the recipient, a tongue
that whipped, words bleeding on
the victim's face, anguish running
down the cheeks and her face,
angelic yet fierce like Joan of Arc

O priestess of the mad, why did
they take you from us, your tongue
prophesied, even in anger or hate
your tongue spoke truth, a prophet
they called you, others said you
were simply mad

Hotel Terminus

There are rules that need to be observed here:
        Not all horses need riders
        Men will take blue rooms
        Women the red rooms
        There shall be no mixing
        Horses must be fed first

The rules are simple here at Hotel Terminus:
        In the morning enter a bus
        the color of your room

        Absolute silence is necessary
        at all times

        When the buses arrive you have
        exactly one hour to dress, pack
        have the morning meal in the dining area

Yes, everything is neon:
        Wild Orange
        Oblivion Blue
        Terminal Yellow

        A hint of eternity to come

Hotel Terminus is strong stone, built by hand
over one hundred years ago by stonecutters and slaves
who labored for freedom which eventually came with
death, hence, the Hotel name

Your rest here tonight is to prepare you for the great
journey

In the morning board a bus the color of your room

Death

Day and time do not matter
        just warm peace
A summer day even in the
        cold of winter

Perhaps it is easy as a
        soft breeze
Quiet and gentle like
        a calm sea
Let us hope the sleep
        is sweet

Texas Tower Massacre

On August 1, 1966 Charles Joseph Whitman, 25,
former Marine and student at the University
of Texas, killed 14 people and wounded 32 others.
Three were killed inside the administration building,
ten were killed from the 29th floor observation deck and
one died a week later from the inflicted wounds.
The tower massacre occurred shortly after Whitman
murdered his wife and mother.

You stand atop the tower on the
observation deck, 29th floor of the
administration building, blood already
on your hands: wife and mother dead

Perhaps it is voices telling you to shoot
or buzzing deafening as people below
walk innocently to work and you look down
seeing useless insects to step on

Crush the people like cockroaches on sidewalks
bullets in place of feet, hands steady rifle
do you – feel close to God or Satan in the tower
up there pulling the trigger again and again

Twenty-five years-old only weeks ago, today you
want to kill one dead for each year but get fourteen, plus
wife and mother, thirty-two wounded before
they get you before the voices stop, the buzzing dies

Blonde, blue-eyes the supremacists would love you,
would send you to do a job they cannot do themselves
and still no clue as to what is inside you, what made you
tick that day atop the clock tower

You fail as a son, husband, Marine, student,
yet you finally find success: fourteen dead,
thirty-two wounded, hundreds with scars of your madness:
were you near God or Satan

Long Dark Night of a Lonely Heart

The heart beat is slow
alone sleeping
it wakes in a crevice
of night unable to
return to rest it
finds a barroom where
the arteries flow with
liquid as the heart seeks
compatibility companionship
false love
where no love exists so it
walks in darkness where
street lamps are broken
or dead of old age
the heart beat increases
the blue veins of night
offering no comfort no hope
no desires fulfilled
the rotted gut of the streets
leaving the heart empty
each chamber compass points
to the oblivion of night
the heart expanding with hope
receding in despair receding
in loneliness stopping at last
beneath a lonely light
under a window

Man With No Shadow

Beware the man with no shadow
He is Death

He follows you until he sees
You without shadow

He takes what he wants
What he wants is you

Cross the portal
Until you are not mortal

Beware the man with no shadow
He is not a vampire

Not ghost nor myth
Just Death

Who seeks you out
For your shadow

Eternal Ocean

Dark ship on a black ocean
races toward infinity
dark sky above moonless
starless a netherworld of
dead seeking eternity
prow pointed north or south
east or west to nowhere
a ship lost among waves
of the last supper or the
morning egg all black like
the black caps of the waves
the black ocean calling

Last Will

He was prepared for death
the family at bedside, shade shut
low lights, the smell of impending
demise, family like vultures gathered
for the feast: money, furniture, books,
paintings, the whole house

The bible on the night table filled with
God's words, if there is a God what
would God think of his life, his loves,
his military career, his many marriages,
his fidelities and infidelities, his greed,
his philanthropy, his regard or disregard for others

He wants to whisper something so the
vultures move in closer, their faces red
with anticipation, glowing with potential
wealth as he coughs and sweats lifting
his head slowly off the pillow, looks at them
and says *Screw you all!*

Unfinished Poem

Her eyes burn intensity
of embers, eerie red, flashes of yellow

The moon moves across the sky
laughing at lovers in the park

The sky folds in like sheets
on a hot day

If you grab the corners
hold tight

Surly Crank

He is dead, the surly crank
Not meeting his maker

Unless you consider Old Beelzebub
The one who gave him his nastiness

His arrogance and affronting manner
His lack of etiquette, Beelzebub

Took his charm and turned it into misery
He will have him

Shoveling coal, breathing fire
and only G–, oops, make that Satan will

Know what is on the menu, who caters
The unappetizing meal of those in his realm

That surly crank is getting his about now
Praying for another chance or the next life

Evil Heart

The Evil Heart is the one on the corner
wearing a green hat with an eagle feather
and a leather band

It looks for trouble, seeking out the
innocent, searching for the dead end
of a walk down a side street

There are those who do not recognize
the Evil Heart when they see it, some know
to stay away, walk the opposite way

The Evil Heart will wander through fields
of overgrown grass or fallen trees looking
to do its evil

For years it will wander toward nothing
until it finds its day of hate, revenge, evil
only then returning to its corner

Stranger

The man at the door is a stranger.
He is not your dead father or your

missing brother. He is not a salesman
or the mailman. Look into the gray eyes

of the stranger and see yourself, see the
future, see the past. The stranger does not

speak, yet you hear the words and see past
the now. More words, then the present.

The stranger turns to leave. The door is shut.
Close your eyes and hope the stranger does not return.

Fear

Old age brings fear, not necessarily
fear of death, only fear of God.

In youth one stands straight, mocks
God curses God denies God, because the

young are indestructible, they pass
a church and spit out chewing gum.

The old have passed through the traffic jam,
as they near their exit, they search for

the brake pedal, they seek to make amends
as their words spill out like milk.

Gothic Fog

On a hot summer when fog hovers
in the graveyard, the musty smell of
the dead rises to meet the Moon,
Queen of the Entombed

She gives them the night to waft
across fields and roads into the
windows of houses and to dance
their nightly gavotte

They enter the unsuspecting
who make love or dream
or enter into the bones of
the growling dog

They fill themselves with the breath
of life so they can live until the next
night and find their own sleep until
roused once more to wander eternally

Land of the Lost

In the Land of the Lost
people walk around with
vacant stares, wander aimlessly
in cities crumbling like cookies
in streets where grass grows
through cracks

Like lemmings they follow each
other into waters of oblivion
over cliffs of the abandoned
lost people with vapid expressions
enthusiasm buried with the dead

They survive on berries and eat grass
drink polluted water and go mad
they are lost in a land of unending
wandering into the void

Nightmare

Walk with padded feet
shoes of cotton and duct tape
sock of spider silk and lemon zest
for the earth opens, ready to swallow

Watch out for the dark where demons lurk
vampire dogs that smell you coming
cats that have not been fed in days
horses galloping to escape carnivores

Welcome the sun and its diseases
deny the moon its sad face
do not worry about being swallowed
the earth always gives up its dead

What Should Have Been

Let me tell you what should have been
What should have been is a blue sky
of sapphires and a red car ripping
open road like a can opener and the man
behind the wheel smiling at its smooth
ride like foam and curves taken like prisoners

But instead, the sky is dark like sunset
clouds gray as disappointed children
and a wet road turns the car into a
spinning top at the second curve and white
horror on the driver's face as he sees
the tree closing in

Horror

Sing loud in the dark
sing hymns, prayers, songs
The flock of evil
descends on steel wings
Beware the cave of no lights
beware the towers of darkness

Sing loud in the dark
sing hymns, prayers, songs
Water rises up from its pool
the sky falls from the heavens
The earth erupts flame
feeds on the living
The days are near
the dead rise to crawl

Street Of No Return

Enter the street narrow as a slice of bread
Bricks worn and cracked
Lined with shops of those who never left

No. 6   rancid restaurant of the starved
No. 18 ark from the exterminated synagogue
No. 19 across the street the gored bullfighter
No. 27 old people with faces of rotting peaches
No. 29 dog barks endlessly

Keep walking in search of a known one
Perhaps your parents or an old lover
Maybe a lost child

No. 33 children died too young
No. 38 widow and abandoned wife
No. 44 holy men of the church crosses on their necks
No. 46 journalists and poets create their fiction
No. 53 politicians still debating taxes

The good and bad share the street
They never leave, they never return
There are sounds of wailing and praying

No. 60 high school graduating class
No. 63 locked door and beauty queens as faded as old drapes
No. 66 chocolate shop with melted sweets
No. 70 bankrupt countess counts her past
No. 96 residence of the black hearted cellist
No. 81 lawyer fat as his wallet pleading his eternal case

And you my friend...

No. 100 waits for you

II. City

City Of Emptiness

I returned to my youth
to the City Of Emptiness

once filled like a water jug
now poured out

Jews gone replaced by
Blacks and Arabs

migrations following migrations
as in many cities an emptiness

of humanity of the heart
followed by hatred

a city of burned memories
demolished hope where

rain runs laughter in gutters
a city of blood and despair

my friends left
gone like stars behind clouds

scattered across new
emptiness where hope

has surrendered and gray
cities crumble like crackers

City of Ghosts

Wooden remainders of a violent past
dirt streets never paved, boot hill's
crumbling stones and echoes of the
past: gunshots of good and bad,
cattle and horses thundering through
streets as cowboys drive their herd
to where tracks remain but there is
no train, no engineer, no passengers
boarding or leaving, just ghosts of
the past looking for each other in
a city that no longer exists.

City Of Gray

Like blind people they grope through
alleys and narrow streets of the city
of the lost – a purgatory of gray
buildings and gray walls, gray alleys
and streets where gray people lead
gray lives and the wanderers seek
happiness in a city that has none as
people in gray uniforms enter and
leave factories with high gray walls
like a prison and their children run
through the streets and never laugh

Nuns march in their gray habits
through gray streets lined with gray stone
buildings with gray sidewalks that even
housemaids in gray uniforms cannot scrub
white like lilies in a window where a
gray child holds a red ball as the nuns with
lines like canals in their faces march to the
gray church in the center of town where
gray mockingbirds sing Gregorian chants

City of Lost Dreams

They come with hope
of a race driver nearing
the finish line
carried by the rush of speed

They come to be dancers, actors
poets, seek the stage of fame
of immortality – filmed, photographed,
pursued, idolized in the city of dreams
where luck and talent is not enough
for of success, where the reality of failure
is despair

City of Dead Cars

They are piled up
each upon the other
two stories high
flattened like crushed
cockroaches
their insides stripped
and sold, rusting automobiles
dead from age
or accident piled high
by the side of the highway
cars zip by, healthy cars
the past rusting like eroding hills

City of Beyond

They enter the dark city
beneath the ground

Workers, shirkers, lovers
criminals

Together they mingle
shadows and wisps

Souls searching for
their home gone from the

Present to a future unknown
a land beyond

Where time ceases
night rules the kingdom

City of Bad Dreams

Dark streets and houses
under a dark gray sky that
pours down black rain

Sidewalks jut up as if
pushed by Satan and
dark blood fills the cracks

A dead cat lies in the
gutter, the dog that chased
it flattened in the street

Rats crawl up from sewers
blind children try to hide
the day becomes black at night

City By The Sea

Waves attack like armies
houses collapse, walls crumble
to a force mightier than the
boulders and streets, turn water
gray as the ocean conquers all
that held it back

Once a resort where people
came for sun, food, swimming,
fortunes built and lost and at
night squeals of love in rooms
with balconies and drapes
floating in waves of wind

They came, built hotels, built
walls to hold back the sea, built
restaurants where the sea offered
its children for dinner, built and
built but the angry sea did not
approve and took it back

City of Night

Night comes in like fingers reaching
for the throat
ragged warnings to save children
legends of vampires and werewolves
shadows crawl in mud
buildings crumble
empty city abandoned to rats and robbers
the homeless
the infirm unable to crawl out of gutters
animals gnaw on the dead
the dying cry *Stay away, stay away*
the lepers of sin roam the streets
Stay away, stay away

City of the Dead

From beneath the sand of four thousand years
the dead rise, tombs of stones and scattered bones
uncovered by wind to let them rise again
the City of the Dead, the forgotten brought not
to life, but remembrance where kings ruled as
gods and people like drone bees built a city for
their king who rewarded them with wars and
starvation and a cruel queen and left their son,
the next king, and his son, the next king who
destroyed his own city for his glory and the
city that slaves built for the king destroyed,
leaving sands to cover it for four millennia

City of Strange Names

We travel to a distant land
a city where steeples rise
like corn stalks and rivers
pour into each other

Streets have strange names
unpronounceable, no vowels
or too many vowels or names so
short only a dwarf would know

Bells ring out more names and
streetcars with abbreviated names
stop traffic and people dodge in
between shouting a strange language

City of the Past

The streets are empty
Tunnels are now catacombs
Buildings where workers toiled
for pennies are tombs, memorials
to their efforts now forgotten
Empty baths, empty brothels
empty temples to the many gods
Only grave robbers and archeologists
care much, learn little while tourists
photograph the dead city as if it
were Paris or London or Chicago

City of Devout

All the religions are gathered in one corner
like stuffed bears in a child's room with
the lights on

The wailing, singing and uttering ring
like bells on a horse pulling a sleigh
in winter

The prayers rising to the unseen god
as if they were balloons with notes
inside unanswered

By day's end wailers, singers and those uttering
return home for a meal where they praise the
unseen god who does not answer

City of Dying

The inventors died
        along with innovators

Cars that ruled the road
        now do not fill a parking lot

What's good for GM is good for America
        Alfred Sloane said while

Henry Ford defamed the same
        Jews who were buying his cars

And Walter Chrysler, not too different
        though his cars were

But now the cars are nearly dead
        vanished makes and models

Muscle cars atrophied
        as the young want luxury

The workers who joined
        the urban flight

Casinos rule downtown
        trains run on crumbling supports

The poor and disabled try
        to win their way to the suburbs

And buy a car no longer built
        in the city that is dying

City of Strangeness

Clocks run backward
steeples bend to the north
the city is slow, people walk
backward, streetcars go
sideways and the children
play hide and seek with
their dogs

When the clock strikes twelve
everyone stops, cars and people
reverse direction, lunch is a meal
taken at the desk or on the streetcar
as the common people watch the
rich in cafes

The river divides the city
those on one side have blue
eyes, the other side brown
though we green eyed tourists
like both

City of Silent Prayers

There is no sunshine, no light
Eyes glow in the dark
Trees cry for their lost leaves
Roses black like coal
The heart measured by dirges
Comfort found on brick beds
Everyone waits for morning
Silent prayers for light
Which never comes, death answers

City of No Longer

You cannot return to a past that no longer exists
        steel mills burned out
        schools torn down
        girlfriends married or long gone
        dead dogs with broken hearts
        streets cracked of old age
        friends forgot you
        empty stores shuttered
        houses where playgrounds were
You can only remember the time and place as if it were
a poster on the bedroom wall or an old movie faded and
crackling, ash of the steel mills still in your nostrils

III. Sorrow Road

Collector of Calamities

He sits in his study reading newspapers
with scissors on the desk
cutting out snippets of random
tragedies

In Montreal, a brick from the 17th
floor of a building falls and hits a
woman eating lunch with her husband
at a sidewalk cafe

A car goes down a highway the wrong way
plows into a family of seven riding
to the beach, all die

Someone does not see a stop sign and strikes
a child in a crosswalk who is walking home
from school

Black and white newsprint cut out, placed
in a bowl, a record of lives extinguished
like flames, a history of calamities by a
collector who has survived big and small
calamities and sees his survival in others' deaths.

Blood Of Affliction

Drink the blood of affliction my friend
drink to those who have died,
gray and buried

Drink to those whose bones are
rotted in a distant jungle, bleached
in the desert

Drink to those who are wounded
whose hearts have become as
dark as a Kafka story

Drink their blood and remember
their names, remember their
affliction and yours

Drink to their women who make
love, whose children despise you
and whose dogs growl at you

Drink to their friends who shun
you and then drink to your own
affliction

Paranoid

The window is shut at night
to keep out the heat of stars
shades closed so the wolf
does not see the vulnerable

The window is shut at night
so the long fingers of trees cannot
ensnare in their master plan to
enslave humanity

The window is shut at night
so screams of deceit do not reach
ears or burning eyes cannot
pierce naked fears

The window is shut at night
so no one will hear ranting
of forgotten lovers, lost dogs
spiders on the wall

Brother

I have no brother
if I did I
would weep
for the one who
does not exist

His face may have been
on every baseball card sent
sailing across a
room to land face
up or against a wall

There is no face to
remember or mourn
no smile to return
no lip to split with
a well placed fist

The brother who does not
exist is the shadow that
follows in the streets
or the rooms I enter
he never cries for me

Bedroom Ghost

as Dickens wrote
perhaps it was a bit of
undigested meat

it might have been
just plain old
imagination at work

when I awoke
in the middle of the
night there it was

black hulk, black ghost
perhaps the grim reaper
or a dead priest in his cassock

it was there alright
a round faceless head
body and arms

shroud floating
out of the bedroom
as I rose to look

floated away, dissipated
evil or good I could not
tell as it disappeared

Sacrilegious

Burning incense, sacrificing a cat
or rabbit to incantations of unknown
words, black robes, red pentagrams
dripping like blood, squealing hamsters
lynched in the basement, the altar of
the holy covered with muslin sheets and tar
they eat raw meat, wash it down with
red wine like blood

She was a fierce, demanding lover
who wanted to conquer everyone she
knew, wanted to control aspects, wanted
to rule the obscene while hidden in her
desk were the papers that told truths
and hid lies she would spend days separating
into drawers labeled by content

When morning rose she discarded black
for conventional attire, went to her job
downtown, sold tickets and seeds, loaned
money to beggars, recruited the poor to
her lair, men and women needing a hot meal,
sometimes they became the meal until she
herself was sacrificed, hanged like a hamster

You Have To Suffer To Be Beautiful

There was the cousin who abused you
when you were only six

At twelve an uncle raped you and
then four high school boys got you drunk

Had sex with you. In college your
boyfriend loaned you out

Then your husband battered you and other
men saw you only for the sex you gave

Do not forget the years of psychiatric hours
to recover and yet, you said when

they asked, *You have to suffer*
to be beautiful

Turn The Handle

You dislike hate, yet you say
you hate everyone who
does not agree – black hole
of politics swallows the enemy
in a meat grinder
words of suspicion turn
the handle with envy –
or is it just hate again
You continue the assault attempting
to convince nonbelievers
you are right, they are wrong
yet you remain loyal to
those who turn bad
as you try to convince
followers that wrong can be right

Shadow Of Death

Crossing the parking lot
a mouse with a piece of bread
scampered out from under a
car darting toward a grassy
area at the near end of the lot.
A hot summer day and I
wondered how the mouse's feet
felt on the hot tarmac, but before
I could complete the thought a
foretelling of death crossed the
mouse turned and a hawk
swooped down, talons extended
then closed as the
hawk gripped the rodent,
who, if it ever wondered what
it would be like to fly, was
getting its wish

Main Street

She pushes a shopping cart
down the yellow line of Main Street
all her possessions packed
in: moth-eaten rolled up rug,
wooden folding chair, slat missing
in the back, two more in the seat,
boom box stuffed in between the rug
and green garbage bag with
clothes scrounged from mission
bins or found in trash or stolen
from another street person,
flip-flops and sandals, half eaten
box of Cheerios – her life in
the cart. She dresses in worn dirty
clothes, pushes the cart down the
yellow line on Main Street while
cars honk, she does not care

Hunger

The rose by another name
does not smell as sweet

the honey seeking bee sting
does not discriminate

the hungry frog can tell the
difference between the fly

and the bee. Its tongue lashes
out like an angry wife, victim

gone, the frog moves on like
an army in search of the enemy.

Seduction

Seduction is for those who want it
        otherwise it is rape

Rape works both ways you know
        he says pleasure, she says hell

Hell is the devil's cup to hold and sip
        an angel's wings to cut

Cut the hot spice of sex into the cup
        to swallow like spit

Spit on those who believe in celibacy
        before marriage or after death

Death may or may not be the end
        does it matter if you are not here and now

Now is the time for the seduction, pick the partner
        do the best to succeed, do not look back

Back to where it all began, a party in some house
        the women having one drink too many

Many women to choose from, picks of the litter
        some reject you, move on, seduction is for those who want it

Long Finger

Death wears a black tuxedo
black shirt, black tie, black
socks and shoes

Death wears nail polish on a
long finger that points to
the black unknown

Death has black teeth
a black gaping mouth
drinks black blood of remorse

Death – black is the black
of long eternity, of wandering
black hallways searching for the right door

Cowards

Come forth from caves
you hide like shivering apes

Come forth to the sunlight
fight like men

Trim beards for us
to see frightened faces, split tongues

Come forth with
orifices emptied

Come forth with robes
covering evil

Come forth to die like men
with Satan in your heart

Come forth to die with sword in hand
vomit in mouths

Heads crushed
like walnuts under boots

Now

Trees wave goodbye to clouds
as you wave farewell
without wings you fly
soaring upward in swirls of dust
returning to an unknown place
among strangers who cross the
river to nowhere

Life is but a series of
crossings: rivers, roads, people
countries where differences
are dangerous and hair is
admired

Close your eyes and imagine
how the past has treated you
the future is the final piece of the puzzle

Ghosts of the Past

In the pajama drawer
is a missing sock

Why its mate was there
months remains a mystery

But together again they are
soul mates

Next time the drawer is opened
a handkerchief and shortwave radio

Appear near the bottom
instructions thrown out long ago

Ghostly happening perhaps resulting
in long deceased parents reappearing near the back

In the closet zippered coat linings discarded years
ago like old lovers, fur moth eaten as many loves

The past bubbles up like La Brea Tar Pits
bones encased in black measured by separation

Inside The Head The War Rages On

Morning jumps up like a baby
and you want to change the
diaper of your life, the woman
who has treated you like a
prisoner of war, the children who
hound as if you are in Baskerville
while the dog you should be
walking has done his thing in the
corner of the living room

Depression comes in four flavors
and you choose vanilla which
happens to be the scent of the
candle she burned when
you found her in your bed with
someone from the Cargo Bar & Grille

You long for the peaceful days of
war in the jungle when
in the heat you smell the enemy
miles away even when they melted
into vines or rocks or hid
in caves and the odor of rotting corpses
that defied the separation of warrior
and civilian denied your senses

Noir
for Gloria

The round face, the happy smile
Words of joy spill like sugar

At night a drop of gloom mixed
With hurt and sadness in a

Meat grinder of poetry where blood
Is black, death is slow

Angels try to save night
From fire and ashes

Hours Gray And Ill

Hours are gray and ill
slipping away like life

Gray turns black
moon gone
stars hide

Sadness pervades
black night, stars hide
from illness of dark

Back Roads

Two lane roads in Tennessee with
farm houses and spots in fields

Cows lazing in sun with rusted pickups
decaying like teeth

Tilled fields waiting for the earth to
give birth while here and there a

Dirt road leads into wood with
signs offering honey or fruits

Once there was a movie about four
young people who followed a dirt road

To a remote cabin where cannibals lived who
ate the people who followed the honey signs

So the dirt road is passed and the gas pedal
is pressed to the floor

National Hooker Night

The whores dance in the streets
It is National Hooker Night

They have the night off to sing
Play games, have fun in the streets

Mexican Hat Dance the song of
Choice and whores laughing

They whirl around packages of condoms
Enjoying clean air of the holiday

Celebrate all night until dawn then sleep
Until the sun sinks like a lead weight

Later they come out, slaves to the night
and the men who seek them

The Whores On St. Botolph

The whores on St. Botolph are
lickin' their chops after a fast $20 job

While restaurant curtains close
so meals are enjoyed

The boys on rooftops with binoculars
and telescopes point to open bedroom windows

Lovers oblivious to the invasion of time and space
continue their passion and sweat, sheets on floor

Pillows cast aside in the name of love
Beethoven's Moonlight fills the room

Eyes wide across the street, giggles and laughs
restaurant empties, whores wait for another Jackson

Night Work

The little women on the corner
sell apples and promises

For a dollar they make predictions
their skirts long, their blouses
sleeveless and wooden clogs for shoes

They would sell themselves for the right
price but nobody wants them, not even
crippled soldiers back from the war or
drunks staggering under streetlights
bathed in fog

The little women on the corner wait until
dawn then eat their apples and go home

Year's End

Final hours of the aged year
snow falls like dying stars
There is hope, why?

We really think the pain,
anguish, anxiety, confusion
will go away with the new year

Like an otter down it slides
an icy slope into a cold river
where little gets clean

and last year hangs out like
freshly washed laundry splattered
with dirt by galloping horses

Dream of the Apocalyptic End
(6 scenarios)

The Bomb is dropped
People look up, mouths open

—

The Bomb is dropped
People look up, scream

—

The Bomb is dropped
People run to basements

—

The Bomb is dropped
Children and animals do not know

—

The Bomb is dropped
Vapor and dust rise

—

The Bomb is dropped
The dream ends

No Vision

One green tree among the bare dead ones
trees pointing up to pray for leaves

Acres of dead cars in scrap yards
Working cars roll by ten miles above the limit

Cemeteries with American colonials under Boston sod
As citizens and tourists walk by looking up

Nude mannequins in store windows stare out
At dressed people who do not notice them

She in a king bed waiting for her lover
who is making love to someone in a double bed

The World Is Ending

The old nun fingers her rosary beads
The old rabbi wears his *tefillin*
They pray and believe
The end of the world has come
Because comedians make fun of the
Crucifixion and the Holocaust
The end of the world has come for
The old nun with her rosary beads
The old rabbi with his *tefillin*
They pray
She for the Church of Remorse
He for the Synagogue of Holocaust Survivors
So much in common
As their world dissolves

Underbelly

I run the gauntlet, home to work, work to home, in between the scum of society, they want my car, my clothes, watch and wallet, they have the look of the starving, the look of the desperate as they grab and grope at every corner where they already have taken street lamps and changed the timing of traffic lights to give them more time for thievery

I have seen them before and can tell you first hand familiarity breeds discontent among the zombies of the homeless, drug infested, hopeless drunkards covered with lice, bitten by bed bugs, feeding on roasted rat or fried mouse, perhaps a stray dog stealing from squirrels chattering protests and trapping pigeons to be stripped and roasted over an open fire under a bridge

I have seen the bottom of the caste, the disheveled and hungry, faces black with soot and ash living in a discarded refrigerator crate, clothes taken from dumpsters, shoes stolen from the dead, found cigarettes dangling from lips encrusted with sores, puss oozing from wounds, coughing their way through the world wrapped in a blanket of holes, a chair missing slats for a throne, toilet under the heavens

I reject the social doctors, the learned, who have answers for those who want no answers, who know what is good for those who want no good and I reject believers more money for those already with money to give to those who want no money, circle of discontent, no familiarity with the true ills of those who live or were born into the unwilling, the uncaring, those satisfied with their lot

I reject the money makers, the ones with green eyes who see only profit as the prophet whose gods are numbered by accounts in banks and stocks and who do not share and do not care about disease, poverty, death and ride by in cars with dark tinted windows not to see the misery of those beneath them, those whom they have treaded on while at their cotillions they dance on the graves of those from whom they sucked wealth

I have no answers I seek no answers, I look with pity upon the
pitiless whom God and his churches have ignored, for religion is
built on money while pulpit mouths spew brimstone and fire of
hell and damnation do not look down to see what is before them:
suffering humanity on a planet of plenty where leaders fighting to
stay in power mouth only words of promise or words of
opposition not offering solutions, only their own political survival

Sorrow Road

I travel down the long highway
Sorrow Road, endless as the sky

The highway where friends
run off the road on the
bumps and potholes of life

There is no shoulder to cry on
or detour of avoidance and no
waves as I pass by

IV. War Zones

War Zones

Jet fighters fly overhead on the
way to a picnic of roast innocents

Mud huts in the desert have no
air conditioning so people bake

Cannibals would feast if they
could leave their jungle mansions

Cows burp grass into the faces of
their killers before becoming dinner

Fish sacrifice themselves to the worm
of the endless fry pan

Vegetables cry when severed from
their stem

Flowers seek revenge following
their amputation from life

And the innocents wail at the loss
of everything as the jet fighters fade

His Life Ended Under A Bridge

His life ends under a bridge
near Pittsburgh
a high school football hero
who joins the army
goes to Nam
kills and is nearly killed
finds solace in drugs
returns home
finds a woman who does drugs
hangs out under bridges
until one day
during an argument
she shoots him in the head
his own pistol from the war –
he dies twice

The Ex-Hippie

Some doped up ex-hippie
living on the street
a tin cup
bought in the dollar store
makes you wonder how they
ever let him in the front door

He sits at the corner of
Congress & Franklin smoking
a joint as cops walk by and know it is
more trouble arresting him than
leaving him there in his camouflage
hat and t-shirt

Every so often someone drops
a nickel or penny in the tin cup and he
nods as dilated pupils squint in daylight
food in his beard dredged from a dumpster
shoes with holes and the wrinkled t-shirt
with peace sign

For a buck he will tell you he skipped
Vietnam for a ticket to Canada worked
on a farm for his drugs grew some of
his own came back with a different
name left a couple kids up there
by two women

A Vietnam vet once kicked the tin cup
scattering the change because he
did not like the ex-hippie's t-shirt and
camouflage outfit but the ex-vet like
the ex-hippie had survived war, drugs and
his own demons

The vet is a business man now in suit
and tie drives a Caddy Escalade has
a wife and three children one in graduate
school one in college one in high school
house in the suburbs two dogs cat
talking parrot

Sometimes the ex-hippie wanders
the streets like a lost cow at midnight
out to the suburbs where
he pisses on the businessman's lawn
in defiance, an infiltration of
the military-industrial elite

One winter he was dead – frozen
a rolled joint still in his hand
the beard a horror of icicles – he was
missed in a police roundup of the
homeless

Red Desert

Blood runs across the desert
like a snake with no tongue

Bones bleached like a Georgia O'Keefe
painting and tanks rumble forward

There are no trees to hide behind
no shelter from airborne bombs

Blood is the oasis of war
the red sun descends on the red desert

A parched tongue, a grasping hand crawls
hot sun and blood make the desert red

No One

People hear but do not listen
Listen but do not hear
Is there a difference

The result confusion
The result ignorance
The result forgotten

Wars happen and
No one listens, no one hears
The warnings

No one hears death
No one listens to death
Even when it enters

Rise Dead

Rise, dead of the Revolution
Departed of 1812 and the Alamo

Keep charging you Gray and Blue
Fight on buried son of Little Big Horn

Rise over there, dead of the War To End All Wars
While World War II's buried sons liberated Europe and Asia

Be not forgotten the frozen of Korea
And rise again you dead of Vietnam

Return to the battlefields of Grenada
Iraq, Kosovo and Afghanistan

Rise and speak of War – of death –
of lost lives – rise and shout PEACE!

A Walk In The Desert

Watch out for booby traps
land mines, snipers, invading
armies, crackle of AK-47s
Under the rocks vipers
scorpions and enemy sharpshooters
You know where the dead are
by the circling vultures
Listen for low flying jet fighters
Beware the sun and the heat
Dress warmly at night
the desert could be the
city where you live

Children Of War

Flat daddy: cardboard cutouts,
something to remind a two
year-old who his father is

No legs, no playing baseball
with his children, he can stand
and hit, but he cannot run

No arms, the son wants baseball
daddy wants soccer. Why? He has
no words

A child watches a friend play
with daddy. He has no daddy
here – only in the casket

For the children of war, when
daddy returns, wounds live on

Arbeit Macht Frei*

Historians said it was the German
sense of humor to place *Arbeit Macht Frei*

at the entrance to Auschwitz, their most
notorious death camp.

Work made no one free at Auschwitz unless, of
course, death is freedom

Then they were free from the miserable slave camps,
the piteous starvation, horrible experiments

on humans, stench of burning flesh
grotesque fall of ash like perverse snow

Listen. Outside more trains are coming.
Achtung. Achtung.

*English translation: "Work Makes You Free"

Ghosts In The Wall
Vietnam Memorial

Ghosts in the wall
behind the wall

looking out at you
you looking in at them

people touching names
with reflections of sorrow

Ghosts speak out
through the names

Ghosts last
through lifetimes

People forget
Ghosts always remind them

ABOUT THE AUTHOR

Zvi A. Sesling has published poetry in numerous magazines both in print and online in the United States, Great Britain, Ireland France, New Zealand, India, Canada, Australia and Israel. Among the publications are: *Midstream, Voices Israel, Saranac Review, New Delta Review, Plainsong, Asphodel, Ibbetson St., Blue Lyre, Door Is Ajar, Scapegoat, The Chaffin Journal, Ship of Fools, Levure Littéraire, The Moth, First Literary Review—East,* and *Main Street Rag.* He was awarded First Prize (2007) in the Reuben Rose International Poetry Competition. In 2008 he was selected to read his poetry at New England/Pen "Discovery" by Boston Poet Laureate Sam Cornish. He was a featured reader in the Jewish Poetry Festival in Brookline, MA. He is a regular reviewer for the *Boston Small Press and Poetry Scene* and is Editor of the *Muddy River Poetry Review* and publisher of Muddy River Books. Sesling has been a featured reader in various venues in the Boston area, San Diego, the Massachusetts Poetry Festival and the Boston Poetry Festival. Sesling has also read on local radio and cable television programs. He is author of *King of the Jungle,* (Ibbetson St., 2010), and a chapbook *Across Stones of Bad Dreams* (Červená Barva Press, 2011). He has taught at Suffolk University, Emerson College and Boston University. He lives in Chestnut Hill, MA with his wife Susan J. Dechter.

www.ingramcontent.com/pod-product-compliance
Lightning Source LLC
Chambersburg PA
CBHW031000090426
42737CB00007B/619